MW01487124

# Rube's Rules for Leadership

Dennis L. Rubin

*Dennis L. Rubin*

*6-9-13*

# Foreword

It has been my distinct privilege to count Chief Dennis Rubin as a friend and colleague for over 30 years. During that time we have shared problems, solutions, ideas (some good, some not so good) as we have moved through our individual fire service carriers.

Most of the time we have worked on opposite sides of the country in very different fire departments. While we both worked in the Metro Phoenix area for a period of time in the 1980's, even that was in vastly different fire departments. My principle reason for pointing this out is that the rules and solutions that Chief Rubin is offering in this book are among those that we have shared and the differences in fire departments, their size or geographic location really didn't matter. What has mattered is that Chief Rubin in moving about the fire service (just a bit) and has had the opportunity to gain those experiences in a variety of fire departments ranging from combination and fully paid, to large Metro and our Nation's Capital, a place where both of us were born and every day brings new, interesting and sometimes very exciting challenges.

The principles being offered in this book are sound personal and professional advice, no matter if you are a newbie or an experienced "old salt" there are lessons to take away with you.

I hope you enjoy reading the book as much as I did and find the offerings worthy of use in your life and organization.

*~Bruce H Varner*

# Introduction

This book is entitled "Rube's Rules For Leadership". It is a collection of "Rube's Rules" that I have put together over the past thirty or so years of my fire - rescue career. I have worked diligently to adopt each and every rule to be a better person, firefighter and leader of men and women. I would say that there is nothing earth shattering about this list of rules that I offer. The significance of this work is my interpretation and application of these rules in every day life. It is my hope that they will keep the reader out of all types of trouble, at and away from their firehouse. However, there is not a day that goes by that we don't hear about a member of our profession that has done something stupid, corrupt, or dumb and is in very serious trouble because of their actions. I wish that I could say that it is only the newest of our firefighters that find themselves in difficult circumstances. But it is the widest range of members from young to old; low ranking to the chief and just about every category of member in between. Hence, the need to review the information in this book regularly. These rules just may keep you and your department out of "hot (in some cases boiling) water." If a member adopts this list as their own, reviews it often and lives by it; I think that they will enjoy a wonderful career without many issues or much drama. I can tell you that when a member "acts out" (does something wrong - morally, legally or against policy), every member in that department suffers. I understand that the pain inflicted is transmitted in varying degrees to each person, but everyone comes out a loser at some level. In fact, I would even go as far to say that the entire fire-rescue service industry takes a hit when anyone of us does something stupid, immoral or dumb.

This small but powerful collection of rules will help everyone to stay on the right course and make our departments proud to call us a "member". There are several ways that you can use the information offered in this little book. First, it is simply just a good read, so take the time to enjoy it for what it is. Next, it will serve as an ever present reminder to go back and review the information inside the covers to stay on top of your "A" game. Finally, for all of those that provide leadership (or are preparing to be a leader) for our members, it is a great format to teach from and discuss with a company, a battalion, a division, or a department. There is an accompanying detailed presentation that will allow you to share the information in "Rube's Rules" with your team members in a formal training setting. This presentation is a powerful way to share the information that is captured in the book. Another suggestion is that the company officer could cover one rule a shift at the dinner table, in an informal and comfortable way. The company boss could have a detailed discussion based on the rule reading and add personal experiences to enrich the discussion, while allowing the other members to add their experiences as well. As a long time fire - rescue practitioner, if I could help a single firefighter avoid a pitfall (minor or major mistake) before they were "jammed -up", I would do so. From every angle, preventing dumb "stuff" from ever happening in the first place, is almost as important as preventing injuries at an emergency incident. This may sound a little overstated, but I firmly believe that it is time to work on our on-duty and off-duty behavior and performance. Just ask anyone that has been in trouble (maybe fired or removed from the rolls of the department as a volunteer member), it is a horrible feeling and to have avoided this problem in the first place would have been a thousand times better than being on the outside.

Safe Firefighting to all and may the God of your beliefs watch over you and your family at all times!

*~Dennis L. Rubin*

# Table of Contents

# Chapter 1:
# You Have to Show Up

*Whatever you do, do it well.*
*~Walt Disney*

After more than four decades in our business, I have developed a list of rules that I try to live by on duty and off duty. Over the years, I kept a list of ideas on three-by-five cards and reviewed the information on them from time to time. Typically, I would pull out the cards when I was preparing for promotional interviews or simply wanted to make sure that I was focusing on what was important to me. The cards served me well, and in great anonymity, until recently.

A fire rescue service mentor asked me to make a presentation on leadership. The specific request was to present my leadership style and philosophies to a national group of senior fire and EMS officers at a staff and command school. That is when I took out the cards and developed a successful presentation based on the rules that I had jotted down over the years. Those that attended the first session of "Rube's Rules: A Leadership Journey" enjoyed the information and provided positive feedback. The rules listed here are in no special order and all are of equal value.

Since then, I have presented this material about a half dozen times, refining the content each time. I thought that it would be valuable to our profession to take the next logical step by documenting them for publication so that more folks could have the benefit of this experience. By no means are these 13 rules new or breakthrough information; they would be best described as time tested leadership points with my personal twist. If you implement them into your daily leadership and management style, I am certain that you will improve your performance as a courageous leader within your organization.

Show up. The first rule seems simple enough, but never underestimate its value or power. Many functions and events occur in, near and around your fire department. By showing up at many of them, you raise your profile and your image within your organization.

Let me start by pointing out that no one in a leadership role should become a "micro" manager; that is, unless the folks being led are new or in need of training and personal development. That information will fall under several other rules. Your presence sends a loud and clear message that you are interested, that you care and that your members are important to you. I have heard this trait referred to by many names, but the most interesting is the "ministry of simply being there." That description has always stuck with me and it makes a lot of sense. I have spent many hours in the hospital with members who didn't know that I was there. However; being present at these critically important times makes a world of difference to those in need and to the entire organization.

Another great benefit of simply "being there" is that it will change some people's behaviors and attitudes and lead them to be more productive. I have attended dozens of community fire and life safety educational events. On the first visit or two, the departmental folks who don't know me spend a little time saying hello and getting the "scoop" on me and what is happening at headquarters. Generally, next we talk about the importance of public education and the role that the members play in connecting the department to the community that we serve.

Then, the members and I discuss how they should perform their duties to leave the best impression possible with our customers. This has always been a very powerful process of street level improvement and acceptance by the members who perceive being "stuck" doing public education. I can recall one specific public education venture. We didn't have any citizens express an interest in accident prevention, so I challenged the crew working this event to "stir up" some interest by asking folks to stop by the Child's Fire and Life Safety House. Before long, the team had a line of children waiting to "Stop, Drop and Roll" and slide down our "Ladder Tower" kiddie slide. What a great improvement, just because the leadership showed a little interest and support of the troops.

Pay attention to details. Another way to measure your impact on an operation is to listen to your operations radio frequency. Over the years, I have worked in cities that followed written guidelines a little closer because a chief officer has started his or her response to an alarm. I can remember as a battalion chief's driver being directed to continue a response to a "food on the stove" report. The chief had me drive to the rear of the structure to ensure that the second in company officer had laid a supply line there, as was required by policy (the chief checking up on a company's position at such a small incident never seemed to happen). As word got out that the newly appointed battalion chief was checking the companies assigned to the rear positions, even on small incidents, the required policy was reinforced and followed closely.

# Chapter 2:
# Lead from the Front

*To Be Effective, Be Sure That Your Actions Match Your Words*

The second rule in this book relates to courageous leadership. Leading from the front is a simple, straight forward behavior that typically can be accomplished mostly with self-discipline and common sense. It is a concept that is easy to understand and easy to write about; however, at times it seems difficult to perform. Interestingly, it seems that it is more difficult to lead by example for long periods, such as the length of a fire rescue service career of 25 or 30 years. With this notion in mind, leading from the front becomes increasingly important to discuss, understand and research further to be successful for the long haul.

There are epic examples of folks saying one thing and doing exactly the opposite. "Do as I say and not as I do" doesn't sell in America and is even weaker in emergency response circles. Do you remember the Arson Investigator John Leonard Orr? He was a highly decorated fire service professional who seemed to be on top of his game in every aspect. He was seemingly a very effective and respected fire captain in Southern California who was revered by many. In fact, Orr was a sought after lecturer and author on the topic of fire and arson investigations. Little did we know the real character of that man who was wearing the firefighter's uniform.

The fire service was amazed to find out that Orr was one of America's most notorious and destructive serial arsonists. He was found guilty of setting dozens of fires up and down the West Coast and was even responsible for several fire fatalities. As Orr would travel to deliver lectures on the topic of investigating arson fires, he would stop along the way and set significant buildings on fire. Then, Orr would "just happen" to be in town after these major events, when he would offer his services to the local fire marshal and he could seemingly do the nearly impossible by determining the cause of the fire quickly, accurately and effectively. I guess it helped that he had set the fires a few hours earlier. After being found guilty by a jury of his peers, Orr is now in a federal penitentiary serving a life sentence for multiple counts of murder and arson.

Put your leadership into practice. To put this rule into the context of your day to day leadership style, everyone in your agency is watching you. The members in your outfit hear you as well, but your actions are what they see, react to and remember. To be a courageous leader by today's standards, your words and your actions must line up and be in sync. As a leader in your department, there can be very little to no difference between what you say you are going to do and what you actually do. The best advice that I can give to you is to determine what your core values are and stick with them.

Most fire rescue department leaders, from senior firefighters to fire chiefs, prepare and circulate a wealth of written documents (memos, emails, member evaluations, reports and the like). The point is that just about every member of the organization can read or hear what you are saying. Your written words have been captured (in some form or another) for all time's sake and your actions (performance) must agree with what you say.

Many years ago, I came across a video that helps me stay focused on understanding the concept of leading from the front. A local TV station produced an undercover news program titled "Men at Work." The program compared public works departments in three communities performing such duties as street repairs and litter removal. Two performed above the viewers' (and media's) expectations. The news reporter raved about the workers, the supervision, the management performance and the government employees in general. Undercover reporting in the third community, however, left viewers wondering whether any work was performed by the public works department or, for that matter, by any city employees. It was an indictment of all government employees – not caring, not performing their required duties and simply violating the public trust.

One supervisor was caught on tape littering and even relieving his bladder in public on the very street he was charged with keeping clean. What were they thinking? What would the results be if the local media spent a day secretly following you and your crew for 12 hours? And, finally, we (the classes and I) have focused on the fact that we (fire and rescue) are a highly scrutinized and highly visible agency. We must always think about how we look to our key stakeholders (citizens and visitors) and always, I mean always, lead from the front.

Always remember that someone is watching you. Whether it is the public, the media or your own people, they are watching!

# Chapter 3: Flawlessly Execute the Basics

*Determine Whether You Are Operating at the Top of Your Game*

In this section of "Rube's Rules", we will discuss ensuring that the job at hand is completed safely, efficiently and effectively. I love the notion of having great customer service in the ways in which we fight fires and save lives. This concept was pioneered roughly 30 years ago by Chief Alan Brunacini (@ChiefBruno); and will be covered in a Rube's Rule later in this book. However, the fact is that we must resolve the emergency at hand quickly and professionally; no ifs, ands or buts accepted.

Before the incident commander can call into the communications center to get the customer service ball rolling, he or she must get the incident under control. I feel obligated to make sure that my opening statement is clear to all. If the fire is still advancing and out of control, but the operational focus is contacting the local Red Cross, the strategic plan is falling apart and out of balance. Obviously, Chief Lloyd Layman's "Big Seven" structural firefighting strategies must be satisfied or at least well underway before related support activities can be implemented.

In order to perform our sworn fire and emergency medical duties, we must be capable of doing the work at hand correctly every time. At a minimum, firefighter/EMTs must be certified to the basic national standards. When I speak of efficiency, one old axiom comes to mind that is a great example: "Extinguish the fire and it will be contained (most of the time) quickly." Of course, you cannot always apply this process, but based on the situation, time, fuel configuration, building construction and the like, there are times when it does hold true. Nothing can ever replace having the correct skills, knowledge and abilities to handle an emergency regardless of whether it is a multi-systems trauma or a second-alarm apartment fire.

Being a big fan of the U.S. military, and in particular the U.S. Marine Corps, I have used a particular phrase to discuss the importance of core values. The slogan is, "Once a Marine, always a rifleman." The point is to focus attention on the core mission of the Marine Corps to protect our nation from foreign and domestic enemies by being an excellent infantryman. As you can tell, this is a very important statement and speaks volumes about being able to flawlessly execute the basics of one's job. In the Marine Corps, whether you are a four-star general or a newly appointed private, you are first a rifleman. The comparison is that if you are going to claim to be a firefighter (regardless of your affiliation – volunteer or career), you must maintain the basic training requirements and certifications to do your job (i.e., EMT, Firefighter 1, Firefighter 2).

During a presentation on leadership, a slide appeared bearing that Marine Corps phrase. A chief officer raised his hand to comment. He came to his feet (a little unusual for a fire-rescue leadership class) and went on to tell an interesting personal story. The chief was a "ring knocker" (graduate) from the U.S. Air Force Academy in Colorado Springs, Colorado. He had done very well in his studies, graduated with honors and received a commission as a second lieutenant in the United States Air Force. The first official act of the new "butter bar" lieutenant was to request a transfer of his commission to the United States Marine Corps. After a few weeks of waiting and a few other administrative steps, he was accepted into the Corps. His first assignment was to be shipped to Parris Island, South Carolina, to learn to be a rifleman, followed by the standard

Officer Candidate School; no shortcuts and a good measure of respect for the core value of being a rifleman. This mission-critical phrase was reinforced that day and continues to keep me focused on just how important it is to "flawlessly execute the basics of your job."

The measurement for all of our credentials (fire, rescue, hazardous materials and the like) should be the same as our emergency medical certifications. I have had the wonderful opportunity to be a part of several Fire-EMS departments in different states over the past few decades. With each opportunity (new department), I was the final authority to determine whether my fire related certifications were acceptable. The state health department (or the equivalent) would review my EMS records and prescribe what training and updated certifications I would need to be a member of the new outfit. Whether it was a required CPR recertification course or a complete NREMT course and testing, it was clear what I had to do to be qualified and certified in the new community. As you can tell, I am very much in favor of national certifications for all of our core disciplines, using the various certification agencies.

The final logical point is to briefly discuss improving your various certifications and capabilities. That is raising the bar as the leader (be it the formal or informal leader) to make sure that you and your department grow and keep up with the changing times. I can remember that in 1971, Private D.L. Rubin was required to successfully complete the American Red Cross Advanced First Aid Course as part of a nine-week firefighter recruit school. This training was great for the times, but within a year it was determined to be outdated and not comprehensive enough for ambulance service. Our department adapted and required emergency medical technician certification as the baseline training. We have never looked back!

Can you imagine never obtaining current training information? This could never happen in the medical world, so I am asking you to make the same commitment in all phases of your career. The National Fire Academy offers one of the best leadership development processes with the Executive Fire Officer Program. This four-year training curriculum touches on all types of strategies to improve your effectiveness as a leader. You should consider obtaining the Institute of Public Safety Excellence's Chief Fire Officer Designation and Chief Medical Officer Designation. These designations are a specific and measurable way to determine whether you are operating at the top of your game and to keep your skills, knowledge and abilities up to national standards. There is no more important function then for a firefighter/EMT to be able to flawlessly perform his or her job when the chips are down. The lives of all first responders and the lives of those in the community that they are sworn to serve are literally on the line every time an emergency vehicle goes out the door.

# Chapter 4:
# Relentless Follow-up

*Liability, Public Trust and Agency Integrity Depend on Meeting Obligations*

I am fortunate to be able to visit a few different fire-EMS departments each year and check out how they operate. From departments on New York's Long Island to the West Coast, it is difficult for me not to stop in and say hello and, if the opportunity exists, to watch as members of the hosting department apply their trade skills.

Universally, I would say that the departments do a great job of following through with the tasks at hand. For instance, when "incident command" calls on the radio for "Division 2" working a hose line fighting fire on the second floor and there is no response, the process is typically consistent from one agency to another. A second radio call is made in an attempt to raise the attention of the operating companies. Once that second attempt is made, usually a Mayday is transmitted and a long list of reactionary steps is taken to locate, protect and remove the companies that are in distress. Fortunately, the root cause of this Mayday rescue activity is a communications problem of one type or another and the operating units were not in too much distress.

The point of this story is that we are great at "relentlessly following up" at most emergency incidents, when our members lives are at risk. However, we get side tracked when less interesting situations occur (perhaps the routine issues are the toughest) and follow-up is a lot more difficult, but still very important organizationally and professionally.

Follow-Up Has Its Rewards

At a seminar on quality improvement, a city manager mentioned that the city that he worked for had received the Malcolm Baldridge Quality Award for being one of the world's best run cities. It was obvious to see the pride in the face and voice of this public-sector executive. After discussing the award for a few minutes, the manager joked and pointed out to the group that among the qualifications that his city possessed was the ability to return the one telephone call that the evaluation team placed to this large southwestern city's switchboard late on a hot summer afternoon. As the Baldridge evaluation team would tell this city manager much later in the evaluation process, 10 calls were placed to 10 major cities around the world in a way that would generate a return call. Only two cities were willing to follow up and learn of the opportunity to be declared one of the world's bestrun cities – and his was one of the two. There were many, many more performance measures that were evaluated and the entire process took over six months to complete, but the very first step to be considered was to simply follow up and return a telephone call.

I had a similar experience when I worked in Atlanta, Georgia. The Fireman's Fund Insurance Company had selected the greater Atlanta area to be the host region for the second phase of the nationwide kickoff of its now very popular Heritage Program. I received a telephone call from one of FFIC's Vice Presidents, Daryl Siry, who wanted to set up a meeting to discuss how his company would provide equipment and other resources for the department and other agencies in the Atlanta metro area.

I was very skeptical about agreeing to hosting this vague planning meeting and the "too good to be true" opportunity caution lamp lit as Mr. Siry described this event. In fact, Mr. Siry had already set up a time and a date that he and his team would arrive at my office to review their plan. Very lucky for Atlanta Fire-Rescue that I was available and able to meet with the Heritage Team with little notice and little background information. Having met with dozens of sales folks, I was thinking that there had to be a "hook" of some type. Well, the FFIC Heritage Program was exactly what Mr. Siry had described. The Atlanta metro area was awarded nearly $500,000 in various grants and Atlanta Fire-Rescue was the recipient of nearly a quarter of a million bucks, simply because we followed up on a request to meet.

Failing to follow up on a specific issue may have results from "no harm, no foul" to disastrous. There are stories of failing to follow up on issues that are of epic proportion and number. When you make a commitment inside or outside your organization, there is always someone that is expecting you to perform the obligation on time and accurately. When an organization fails to follow through with a commitment, no excuses are acceptable to regain the public trust that is lost.

The District of Columbia Fire and Emergency Medical Services Department had a very aggressive smoke and carbon monoxide detector installation program, during my watch. As the former fire chief, some of the worst news I can get is that we committed to installing a detector and failed to complete the task in the timeline agreed to with our customer. Concerns like liability, public trust and agency integrity all came into question when we fail to meet our obligation. The senior officers who oversee this program were regularly reminded of the importance and consequence of failing to meet the agreed schedule. Further, I conducted spot checks on our "Smoke Detector" hotline at least monthly.

# Chapter 5: Communicate

## *The Art of Learning How to Communicate at Emergency Incidents*

Without a doubt, the process of communicating is critical in every phase of emergency services work. Interestingly enough, how effective we are at communicating on the emergency scene will likely determine the success or failure of our operations. In fact, next to operational tactics, strategy, and execution; proper and effective communications are likely the next most important process that we engage in performing. When communications are effective all seems to go well and when they don't, disaster occurs just about every time.

There are brilliant case studies that identify examples of great communications and other case studies that describe very, very poor ones. Both will be explored in this section, along with ways to ensure that your critical communications processes are effective. Non-emergency situations require effective communications as well, but the focus of this section will be that of what happens while we are working on the streets.

The $64,000 question to be considered is whether two people can have perfect communications under ideal conditions. As you have likely guessed, this is a trick question. A hint: Are you married or do you have any teenagers at home? Usually, these notions elicit a chuckle or two from most folks, understanding that the process of perfect communications is difficult at best even under ideal conditions. Starting with the basic idea of communicating an idea or thought is developed by a person sending (sender) a message to another person (receiver). This message must travel through some sort of medium, perhaps a portable radio, to the receiving person. Generally, there is some sort of interference (background noise, accents, volume to mention just a few) that degrades the quality of the message. Then the receiving person has to decode the message to provide feedback or take action.

Here's a personal example. In 1990, my son was in the final approach to graduate from high school. He was a good student (B's and C's), a quality athlete and in general a very well-behaved young man. Well, at about T-minus six weeks, my son asked me to buy him a car to reward him for his efforts of twelve years of schooling. Needless to say, I agreed with very little thought, knowing that he had performed so well.

In the flash of the instant of me saying yes to his request, he was envisioning sporting around in a Corvette or perhaps it was a Porsche or some equally exotic and expensive automobile. I had clearly thought that the family VW Bug would be the ticket. Perhaps with new paint, tires, brakes and a little body work, I would be able to provide him with great transportation for an investment of about $1,000. Needless to say, we were both taken aback (a lot for me) in trying to understand each other's concept of a graduation gift. Had our communications failed? The compromise was a pickup truck that was a few years old and bought from a local car dealer.

Now, I must ask, do you think that my namesake was wearing a face-piece and talking to me through an 800-MHz portable radio? Dennis was not crawling through smoke or under great stress in an immediately dangerous to life and health (IDLH) atmosphere while he was communicating with me. Think back to the situation of the discussion; it was under ideal and relaxed conditions. Neither the sender nor the receiver had to compete with screaming sirens or roaring diesel engines. I assure you that there was no breaking glass, smoke detectors or squealing fire alarm systems providing interference noises.

When we communicate at most alarms, all the above factors must be considered and overcome for us to be effective at the mission-critical function of communications. Transmit your message in a concise, clear, calm and commanding (projected, but not screaming) voice. When the transmit key is activated, pause for just a fraction of a second so that (hopefully) your radio will capture the signal, ensuring that the entire statement is heard by all on the alarm. Next, always use standard messages and directions that are incorporated into your department's policy and training. All operational communications must be based on the National Incident Management System (NIMS) model, following the protocols. The day of the "10 codes" and other coded messages have gone the way of the horse drawn hose wagons (although those were the good old days!) Plain text messages are a necessity for all response agencies, including the police department. No worries about a missed interrupted code or a misunderstood one with the plain talk text.

Perhaps the most important concept is that of using the communications order model all the time. Always briefly, but accurately, repeat the message to ensure understanding and reception of the message. When command gives the order to a truck company to provide positive-pressure ventilation to the fire floor, the truck company assigned must restate the chief 's message to ensure that communications has successfully occurred. "Copy," "Received," "OK" or any other limited acknowledgment is just a communications trap waiting to bite an officer. Take the time to briefly restate the core idea of the message to make sure that the direction was received and understood. "Command to Engine 25." "Engine 25. Go with your message, Command." "Engine 25. Advance a 2 1/2-inch handline to the second-floor bedroom in quadrant C – Charles and attack the fire. You are assigned as Division 2 supervisor." "Engine 25 copies. Advance a 2 1/2-inch handline to second-floor bedroom on quadrant C – Charles and attack the fire and assume Division 2 supervisor." "Affirmative Engine 25." The complete idea has been communicated from one person to another with a high degree of understanding.

A running complaint that I hear about using the communications order model is that there is not enough radio time or personnel to use such an elaborate process to get a simple task communicated. The reality is that you can't afford not to use this system, which is intended to prevent mistakes, omissions or duplications of tasks. The last thought for this section is to remember to use the phonetic alphabet when communicating, such as C as in "Charlie", as in the above example. By using the phonetic pronunciation, understanding will be greatly increased and confusion and misunderstanding limited.

There is an art to learning how to communicate at an emergency incident. There is a great deal of stress and other negative factors that must be resolved to be an effective communicator. Please take the time to learn more about effective communications and training on all of your department's policies and procedures as though your life depends on it, because it does!

# Chapter 6:
# Consistent Performance

*Consistency Must Include the Ability to Perform Correctly and Effectively*

Perhaps the most important trait for any organization is consistent performance in every aspect of its operation. I cannot think of a single agency that doesn't want to be consistent in how it functions and delivers services or products to its customers.

The American fire-rescue service is no different. A comment that a fire chief hates to hear is several or even many fire departments are operating under the banner of his or her agency. For example, seven battalions times three shifts could equal 21 small departments within one agency. Some outfits devote a lot of time to achieving and measuring their performance to ensure that they are consistent in all that they do. Few departments place little or no emphasis on consistent performance, and they pay for this behavior at an emergency incident.

Consistency must include the ability to perform correctly, effectively and safely. We in the fire-rescue service must strive for consistently great performance because lives depend on our services. A department's strategic vision should call for consistently great performance by all members and companies all of the time and provide a way to measure the results. This organizational goal is simple to recite and understand, but it is difficult for any agency to achieve, much less one that must work under demanding constraints all of the time.

If Standard Operating Procedures (SOPs) or even the style of hose loads are based on the shift that is working that day, true consistent performance will be difficult to impossible to reach. In some places, core operations change in measurable and visible ways from one shift to another. If there is a void in operational procedures, if training to support the procedures is not sustainable and in place, or if an agency's policies are not enforced, the outfit will never attain consistently good performance. All of these elements must be in place, described officially and supported organizationally all of the time if the agency is to achieve this highly desirable outcome. In fact, a reward system must be established around attainment of consistency. If the leadership of the agency fails to set standards and provide the needed resources and incentives, the department is destined to varying results and varying community satisfaction levels.

To underscore the importance of this organizational goal, let's talk about an American institution that exudes consistency in products and performance. Many years ago, when Ray Kroc and the McDonald Brothers put forth the concept of a fast food hamburger restaurant, their core value would become consistency. Think about the last time you visited a McDonald's restaurant near your home. Then, think about the last time you visited a McDonald's more than 100 miles from your home. What was that experience like? I would be willing to guess that the visit was just like the one at your home-based McDonald's.

I would submit that you enjoy the same tastes, flavors and textures at the remote location as at your home "Mickey D's". I would further venture to say that the restaurant was reasonably clean with customer service that you have grown to expect from this giant corporation. I am thinking that the pricing was roughly the same, as were the shape and size of the parking lot.

Early into this great economic venture, the management structure figured out that consistency was the way that

McDonald's would be a highly profitable corporation. About five decades later, the company is thriving and is a model for consistent performance. The company spends a great deal of time and energy to ensure that a customer's dining experience is a controlled and expected one. We could learn a lot from the model that this fast food outlet provides for us.

The consistency journey should start with the development of clear, concise and well-written policies. Some organizations are reluctant to place their policies into a written format due to the legal concerns. The arguments stems around the belief that if policies, procedures or protocols are committed to paper, the agency could be held accountable for substandard performance in a court of law. In fact, there is an element of fire chiefs who think that the documents need to be described as "guidelines," not procedures. Regardless of the name selected for the organizational directives, they will have to be memorialized in print and available for frequent reference.

Next, there must be a formal way of learning and sustaining the information by the members of the department who will be delivering services to the public. Often, organizations develop an initial officer training program and the follow-up retention training is left up to chance. The best systems that focus on consistent process incorporate an ongoing training component that makes sure that the mission-critical information is renewed and reviewed on a regular basis.

The last step that helps to ensure consistent performance is a follow-up and/or enforcement component. The best position that a chief could hope for, is figuring out a reward system. Because all of the members are following the policies, procedures and protocols every time and need only positive reinforcement for their work. The reality is, however, that sometimes we all must be guided toward compliance. A standard, clear, transparent, fair and equitable follow-up system should be developed and implemented to keep the agency focused on consistent high quality performance.

When I discuss consistency, I must include a comment about using job aides to ensure that we get the task at hand completed correctly the first, every time. In 2008, the District of Columbia Fire & EMS Department had just implemented a structural fire and special operations "Job Aide" that let responding companies complete a quick reference while responding to a specific type of alarm. The concept is that an officer can complete a last minute check to ensure that all elements of a particular pre-determined assignment are handled correctly on every single response (consistent behavior/performance).

We use several checklists during emergency events that keep us focused like a laser during immediately dangerous to life and health (IDLH) operations. After several rounds of Mayday training evolutions, a useful and effective Mayday checklist was finalized and added to the resources that the incident commander has at his or her disposal at the command post. Finally, a "mini" operational critique is conducted after each working incident, while still on location and before the units are allowed to return to service, to discuss whether we followed our policies at each significant event. This procedure, developed by a great operations commander, Chief Lawrence Schultz, has had amazing impact and results to help us ensure consistent perfect operational performance.

# Chapter 7:
# Tell the Truth, Always

*The Art of Learning How to Communicate at Emergency Incidents*

The next rule is perhaps the simplest to understand and you have heard it many times and from many different folks throughout your life. Tell the entire truth the first time and every time that you are asked. Understanding that our most precious resource is our people and that our people are human, the possibility does exist for deception, so it makes sense to talk about it in the rules. It seems like quite the irony that the folks that Americans trust the most, firefighters and paramedics, can sometimes withhold information, mislead or otherwise not be truthful in the workplace.

To capture and maintain the public's trust is one of the most important functions that a fire department can perform. To perform our jobs properly, the public must have a high degree of trust in every aspect of our abilities. Considering that a firefighter has more "position" authority than does a police officer, it is clear that we must maintain and protect the public's trust.

In our nation today, firefighters from coast to coast will enter homes without search warrants to handle a wide variety of fire and medical emergencies. Paramedics will be required to cut away clothing from unconscious and unresponsive patients to perform required and needed emergency medical services care. Many of these folks in distress will not be accompanied, so their fate (health and safety) is in our hands. These mission critical tasks can be performed only if the level of public trust is high enough, in your city and mine, to support the performance of your jobs.

One way that we can help to ensure that we have the faith, trust and support of the public is to simply be truthful with them all of the time. During one of the previous presidential administrations, the phrase was used that "the best disinfectant is sunlight." The meaning of this metaphor is that whatever action a public person or agency is taking should be completed in a way that everyone can see all of the elements of the process and there are no surprises for anyone, especially the public. Once public trust is called into question, it is difficult for the department to reclaim the trust that it once enjoyed.

A major component of this process is for all of our members to believe in the core value is "telling the truth, the whole truth and telling it the first time." Without fail, we all will be guilty of making mistakes from time to time. That is part of the human nature of being mortal. In fact, the philosopher Cicero in 43 B.C. wrote that "to err is human," so we have been making honest mistakes for a long, long time. Where the train jumps the tracks and the trust in the department slips is when we try to cover up or hide a mistake. Nothing could hurt your organization's reputation and standing in the community more than to have willfully mislead the public that you are sworn to serve and protect.

Most folks understand that honest mistakes will be made from time to time by nearly everyone. The best action that can be taken in this difficult situation is to acknowledge the mistake, investigate why it happened and put controls into effect that will at least likely eliminate or avoid the mistake in the future. First, if you don't acknowledge that a mistake was made, there is very little hope that corrective and preventative action can be implemented. Next, any action that tries to minimize or redirect the blame is a step that will be clear to all and seen as a hollow attempt to resolve the issue. Finally, deliberately misleading or misguiding the public on a topic will come with great organizational danger and consequences.

Understanding modern day communications and investigation techniques, it is very unlikely that a significant issue can be kept secret for a long time anyway. So, take your medicine on the front end of a problem or issue by getting out in front of it early and being honest. It is amazing how effective you will become at protecting the public trust that your agency desperately needs and the issue will get smaller over time instead of becoming larger. People can accept mistakes; by and large, they will not tolerate liars.

Sometimes, the issue at hand is a simple personnel-related problem, such as arriving to work late. Most every firefighter would relate to this situation occurring and can likely describe some personal event that caused him or her to miss the start of "line-up" (shift change). No one likes to be in trouble or embarrassed in the workplace, so it is understandable why a person may think that manufacturing a story to save face is a good alternative to a bad situation. However, don't take that path! You will regret it in the long run and risk a much more severe penalty when the truth surfaces. The truth always seems to come out eventually and lies are very difficult to remember. In most outfits, coming to work late a time or two means a written reprimand or short-term suspension – not a pleasant experience, no doubt, but survivable. The best advice that I can give you is to "Firefighter Up" by admitting the mistake and taking the consequences that you have earned. And, of course, don't be late to work anymore (change the poor behavior!)

On many occasions, folks have tried to "sharp shoot" the system and lie their way through an issue. The end result typically is a harsher punishment. Some agencies have rules that are grounds for termination for the act of lying, lack of candor or misleading an investigation.

The ability to simply tell the truth is instilled into all of us. If your practice is to always follow this rule, your life will be a lot simpler and your organization will be able to capture and maintain the public's trust in everything that you do. Once a person goes down the path of deceit, it is tough to recover from and almost always makes a bad situation much worse.

# Chapter 8:
# Do the Tough Stuff First

*Stay Focused and Prioritize Your Shift Time Early*

The choice to select the day's work activities is typically made by the company officer at the beginning of each shift. In fact, the list of duties is generally left up to the station/company commander with the exception of emergency responses and some planned events such as designated training exercises that are scheduled by a higher authority. Tough questions for the "boss" are what does the daily activity plan look like and what should be accomplished during the company's tour of duty for the next 12 or 24 hours? Seems like such a straightforward and simple question, but the variance in accomplishments (lack of consistency) between shifts and officers is mind boggling.

Most companies will make the most of a shift/duty day, while others may not be as successful in being as productive. Finding and maintaining a workload balance is a leadership art unto itself, as most supervisors quickly recognize. But one thing is for certain - if you tackle the difficult items at the beginning of the shift, they are exponentially likely to get completed in a timely fashion, rather than being put on hold until later. The time-tested adage, "Don't put off until tomorrow what you can do today," comes to mind when I discuss the faults of procrastination.

There are many responsibilities and duties that are not pleasant or very desirable. As a firefighter, washing windows was one of those dreaded tasks that I never looked forward to being assigned to accomplish. In fact, I would attempt to "swap" house chores with another member (with little or no luck) whenever the windows were assigned for me to clean. It was always much easier to complete the house duties that

I enjoyed (i.e., preparing the apparatus for response) and seemed to me to make a difference.

As a private (firefighter rank nowadays), I would even report for duty a bit earlier than my colleagues to ensure a better chance of being assigned more compatible house duties than those dreaded windows. However, I occasionally found myself with an assignment that was simply no fun. The older members would make encouraging statements like, "Take the bitter with the sweet, Rookie." Of course, those were the same folks who would work their hardest to make sure that all of the members were assigned tasks that they didn't necessarily enjoy completing.

If left to my own devices, I would have liked to swap duties (no doubt) or procrastinate and not start the hard stuff on that day. Either the task would be assigned to next shift or the windows would become filthy under the "Private Rubin House Duties Plan." Needless to say, neither passing off the work nor not doing the required cleaning was an option, so I would reluctantly go about my duties when required to do the less glamorous tasks. You could only wait for a working fire or "mega-trauma" code for so long before it was obvious that you were sloughing off your duties.

As I became a little more senior in my position and when I started up that promotion ladder, the harsh reality of having too much work to complete in one shift became abundantly clear. The need to develop a priority system and to put the shift into some type of logical order was apparent. For a short while, I would go after the low-hanging fruit (easy stuff) and completely fill my day. That seemed to keep the higher bosses as well as my crew happy. However, when mandated projects were slipping through the cracks that I was causing, the less than desirable performance was noticed and a heart-to-heart discussion was held with the higher ups and this company officer. That was just about the time that I hit on the need to do the tough stuff first and meet all of my deadlines, not just the fun tasks. What a valuable lesson that I learned many years ago: Get the tough stuff behind you early in the shift.

Later in my career as a chief officer, I hated dealing with the end point of the discipline process (employee termination). It always felt like the department had failed by hiring the wrong person in the first place or by not being able to reach the member with improvement programs before it was too late to save a career.

The tendency was to leave perceived "difficult job assignments" until the last possible time. Oddly enough, waiting to deliver bad news (about discipline or anything) never made the information better or easier for me to deliver. It just added to the agony of being the bearer of the unpleasant fact of process. It took a while, but I realized that this was not helping anyone and that handling the difficult personnel issues in a timely fashion was the only way to deal fairly with this difficult duty.

If you complete the tough jobs at the first of your shift, the day will get easier as you go. I understand that this rule is a blinding flash of the obvious, but it is important enough to remind everyone of its value and power. As a direct result of taking the tough issues head-on, you will develop a solid reputation as a person who is a high performer and can prioritize properly, keeping the organization's needs ahead of your own.

I signed up to be able to help people and for all of the excitement and challenge. If I had the fortitude to complete the less desirable or more difficult assignments before the action packed events occurred, that made for a wonderful day at work. However, when I would let things get out of balance (fail to handle the tough stuff early), difficult times always seemed to be just around the corner. I can't count the number of times that I have completed budget documents on a weekend or stayed over late to complete personnel evaluation forms that were required for a member to receive a timely pay increase because an emergency event took up all of my shift time.

# Chapter 9:
# Be the Customer Service Advocate

*Opportunities to Add Value to What We Do Every Day Are Endless*

No set of rules could be complete without discussing the need for and the application of customer service. It is amazing how times have changed and along with that so must our focus. When I first started in the department in late 1971, the "customer" was clearly seen as the emergency event. It seemed like it was almost painful and disrespectful to talk directly to our real customers (the humans) that were having a really bad day.

In some ways, the people associated with the problem were seen as an impediment to resolving the emergency at hand, and not somebody that we would ever talk to or comfort during our operations. As a young firefighter, it was a lot simpler dealing with just the emergency event. Apparently, there wasn't a need to interact with the people that were in great distress; perhaps that was the job of the police. I would say that we went to great lengths to separate the people that were suffering through an event from the event itself.

I can remember heading off to a car fire that occurred on a limited access highway. That was very exciting! The large, billowing column of thick, black, highly carbonaceous smoke could be seen for miles. The traffic had been stopped by our police partners and our folks were focused on the action like a laser beam. We were riding in on the BRT (big red truck) to save the day, just like it should be, "textbook style." Our supply hose line was laid to one of the many hydrant access points on this highway and the attack line was stretched just like we were taught to do. Poetry in motion. This time, there was a big crowd of people (perhaps this was because of the time of day, the location and billowing smoke cloud) and we needed to be perfect under such public scrutiny.

As the operation progressed, the fire was knocked down in just a few minutes and the smoke's intensity died as the flames diminished. The "layout" person moved into position to open the hood with the assistance of the lieutenant using the flat-head axe and Halligan tool. The tactics of the day were going well at this point. So far, so good, as the raging car fire was extinguished. After opening the hood, which exposed the bulk of the fire, the same two members moved to force open the trunk and interior to check for fire extension in those compartments as well. Inside of four minutes or so, we had the upper hand on this blaze, and as always, it felt good to "tame the beast."

You likely can guess what happened next. The members of the engine crew completed a thorough overhaul of this once nice looking Chevy, making sure that the fire was completely extinguished. Then, we (the remainder of the crew) cleaned up our tools and appliances, using the booster line, while we waited for the fire investigators to arrive. Our officer spoke to the passengers of the barbecued automobile to obtain the basic information (name, address, insurance, etc.) for the all important fire report preparation. Within the next 30 minutes or so, I was standing on the dirty 11/2-inch hose rolls on the back step (not so bright, but remember the era) headed back to quarters to finish the job of being ready to respond to the next alarm.

About the only thought that we had about the people involved in this vignette was the thought that we hoped they didn't get hit by other cars while they stood out on a high-speed road. The ambulance crew was always busy and they didn't need any more calls for service that day. There you have it, another satisfied customer! Or so we thought.

We extinguished their car fire in minutes and had only a few seconds of discussion and interaction with the "victims." And, the last act of "their" fire department, when we departed, was to cover this stunned older couple in a cloud of diesel exhaust. Now that should be pleasing "customer service" to any taxpaying citizen. How can you not love the firefighters that are willing to risk their lives to save your property from destruction, and don't have hardly a word to say to you, or even help you out of a bad situation?

When this situation presents itself, we should have a completely different and more comprehensive approach to solving customer service needs. First, we need to properly and quickly resolve any emergency situation by flawlessly executing the basics of our job (see "Rule 3: Flawlessly Execute the Basics"). Once we have the upper hand at resolving the situation, we must focus on the people that are directly and sometimes indirectly involved in getting through and recovering from the emergency. This means that the focus must become helping the humans that are impacted and the only way that we can do that is to open a line of professional, but frank communication. Most folks will not have a lot of experience at calling on your services. This will likely be the first and hopefully the last time they are users of your community's response system. So, try to make a lasting great first impression with your skills, knowledge, abilities and professional demeanor.

Going back to the car fire case study, consider if we had taken a few extra minutes to pack up the couple and take them to a place where they could get the help they needed. The list of immediate issues that needed resolution was very obvious to get those folks back on track. The unlucky couple needed a place to get out of the traffic, use a telephone (before cell phones were in general use) to call their insurance company, and call to have their car towed and repaired. And finally, a way to connect to a replacement rental car to complete their trip and regain control of their situation. It is no big deal to help with any one or all of these items and it is the right thing to do.

How times change! It seemed like life was so much simpler when we didn't have to interact so much with the people we serve. But when you think about the work that we do and the close connection we must build with the people experiencing an emergency, it just makes good sense to provide for the needs of our customers in a more direct and personal way. The above case study simplifies the general philosophy that needs to be applied; however, the opportunities to add value to what we do every day are endless.

I guess we have Chief Alan Brunacini to blame (actual thank) for this dramatic change for the better. And, once your organization takes and truly embraces the customer service journey, the rewards will be amazing. They will first appear as kind notes and letters and ultimately as support in the all important political arena. Never lose sight of the fact (political arena) is how we get our funding.

# Chapter 10:
# A Passion for Health and Safety

*We as Firefighters Can't Help Anyone Else If We Need Help Ourselves*

Great leaders must ensure that all firefighters go home at the end of an alarm or shift. This rule is the most important one in the entire list of Rube's Rules for Leadership.

To define "Everyone Goes Home" a bit more, our members must return to their families and homes just as they arrived at the firehouse, before the response to an event or the completion of a shift. The fire-rescue department exists to help others during their difficult time of need, the notion is that we must be able to help folks when, where and how their situation demands. We perform on the street as the situation generally dictates. There are only a few times that we react to the conditions that are presented to us by trying to change them, such as holding a defensive position until the police can control a hostile scene.

If we are not physically and mentally able to do so, we will fail at the mission that we are sworn to carry out protecting the public that we serve. Without the required human resources to perform that work at hand, simply put we will not be successful. Our industry is and will forever likely be highly dependent on people to carry out the required tasks to save lives, protect property and help secure our homeland.

One of the most heroic case studies that I can share is the tragic event best known as "Caught Under the Wheels." In the 1980s, a young, capable firefighter was on duty assigned to a ladder truck in Prince George's County, Maryland. During the evening of the shift, a box-alarm assignment was dispatched for an apartment house on fire. Firefighter Sandy Lee quickly reported to her assigned position of the right jump seat on Truck 22 and mounted the apparatus in preparation to respond to this call for help. However, Firefighter Lee skipped the step in donning her turnout gear and failed to use the seatbelt that was provided to protect her.

As the response started and the ladder truck began to move, Sandy's turnout boot fell from the jump seat (back in the days of three-quarter boots and open jump seats) onto the concrete ramp in front of the station. A natural reflex was to reach for the boot. In a split second, Sandy fell from the vehicle onto the ramp. With the siren and air horns sounding, her screams for help and for the vehicle to stop went unheard. As you might have guessed, Sandy was struck by the tandem rear wheels of the ladder truck. She was dragged more than 30 feet across the front ramp and sustained severe damage to her body. This event would change her life and career forever.

In fact, Firefighter Lee was the first transported to the Prince George's General Hospital (PGGH) Level 1 Trauma Unit for stabilization. Soon after being stabilized at PGGH, Sandy was flown to Baltimore's Shock Trauma Unit. The staff there was able to somehow miraculously save her life from the threat of such devastating injuries. Requiring dozens of operations and hundreds of pints of blood transfusions, it was a miracle that she did somehow survive this traumatic ordeal.

As her healing along with the physical and mental rehabilitation process started, Sandy developed an amazing training program that she entitled, "Caught Under the Wheels." In retelling her story scores of times, Sandy would make firefighters think about following their department rules (donning turnouts before the response) and to always use their seat belts before the vehicle starts into motion. There are several very powerful videotape presentations in which Firefighter Lee appears with the goal of making sure that this information is not be lost on future generations of firefighters.

As this overwhelming powerful presentation concludes, Sandy takes full responsibility for her actions. She goes on to say that because of her accident, the ladder truck that she was assigned to that night never made it to the apartment fire. Further, because of her, the medic unit and the battalion chief assigned to assist at the apartment fire never made it as well. Of course, they were all assisting with the injured firefighter who was down on the front ramp of Station 22 that night.

Sandy will always hold a special place in my heart and thoughts. This is not just because she sustained career-ending injuries and immeasurable suffering that night while protecting her community. In addition to being such a courageous leader and hometown hero, Sandy developed a behavior-modifying training program and she did something few folks do today at any level of our society – she took personal responsibility and accountability for her actions.

I think of Sandy often and I shall never forget the sacrifices and contributions that she has made to the American fire rescue service. When I discuss firefighter safety, I use this example to make folks think through the fact that you can't help anyone if you are hurt. Hopefully, you have never experienced a member being injured during an operation. The folks who have had this unfortunate event occur can fully appreciate my next thought. The entire company that you are working with goes out of service when a member is injured. In fact, if the injury is moderate or more significant, other companies will be called in to assist by providing medial aid and transportation to the downed firefighter. Once this process unfolds, it gets more difficult to resolve the situation that we were called on to handle in the first place. The very nature of this type of alarm gets more dangerous for all hands at this point.

There are dozens of great firefighter safety and survival programs readily available. The National Fire Academy (NFA) is a great place to start or continue your lifelong educational commitment to firefighter safety. You should consider taking the NFA's on or off campus firefighter safety programs. Each day, more information appears on the web and is increasingly easier to access to improve our operations from a member safety standpoint.

Please take the time to make a concerted effort to learn more, all of the time, about this critical topic. If you are a company or chief officer, your responsibilities to this process (member safety) exponentially increases. Never forget your first duty as a leader of our people, and that of course is to their safety. The entire operational process depends on being able to deploy members who are capable of performing their assigned duties. All officers should obtain and maintain the national incident safety officer certification to be able to perform their duties correctly. You owe it to your family, yourself and your department to "go home" after every run or shift. Please be safe out there!

# Chapter 11:
# If You Don't Care, Get Out

*Tips to Help You Avoid Falling Into the "Apathy Trap"*

One of the most difficult personnel issues is how to stop members from falling into the "apathy trap" once they decide that they don't care about the agency any longer. When a member acts out that they "don't care" about the department or projects harmful behavior to other members or, heaven forbid, to customers, a lot of organizational damage can occur. The "fix" becomes a slippery slope that can damage both the organization and the member.

This section reflects a sincere desire and need to keep your folks engaged and productive throughout their career or affiliation with the department. It is amazing to see how infectious a positive attitude toward the community and our service can be, in direct contrast to how harmful lackadaisical and uninterested behavior can become.

I like to ask the most disgruntled employees to take a journey back in time to when they were appointed to the position of firefighter or "voted in" as a volunteer member. If the person is willing to step back with me, there are vivid memories of great community and departmental respect and support. Perhaps during the interview process, the disconnected members made statements about their willingness to take on assignments that they are asked to do whenever and whatever the task involved.

In fact, let's go back in your career for a moment. What was it like when you first realized that you were going to be a protector of your community? My guess is that it was a daunting and exciting feeling. Most folks would remember that time and what it felt like to ride on the big red truck for the first time. I remember the date, time and address of my first response: September 9, 1968, at 8:30 P.M. for smoke in the building at the Prince George's Plaza in Hyattsville, Maryland, riding the back step on Engine 12. For me, this was the end of an eight-year wait to be a "riding member," so I am sure you can imagine my excitement and enthusiasm.

Now let's move the clock to today. What is the "condition of your condition" (your organizational attitude and core value system)? I hope it is the same as it was on your first day in recruit school or when you responded to your first alarm. However, if it is not, what will it take to get you back to that place? Who has control over your morale? Who determines at what level you can participate and contribute within your organization? Who is directly responsible for your personal performance on and off of the job? Who can instill a sense of departmental pride and support? Who can make sure that you are self-disciplined and that you stay out of trouble? Who can make sure that you are completely capable to perform the job well and maintain all of your certifications?

Of course, the answer to all of those questions is you. Others can try to influence your actions, decisions and behaviors, but you are in control of your destiny within your agency and in your life. You have the free will to choose your course and project the attitude and actions that you desire. In fact, the more professional and self-disciplined that you are willing to act within your department during stressful times, the more likely you are to be insulated from the potential negative forces that enter into everyone's life from time to time.

Most folks want to be around people who project a positive attitude and image, rather than deal with those who have a lot of baggage and attempt to bring those around them and the organization down to their level. Don't let negative energy get a foothold on you, it will be tough to shake it off. There are many ways to deal with a bad day or even a bad week or year. Perhaps take a vacation, even a "mini" one, to bring about a change of attitude. Communicate your concerns with someone – your supervisor, personal mentor, spouse or spiritual advisor – to get a change of focus and an adjustment of attitude. Try to think about the importance and value of your role within the department and the mission-critical work you do for your community.

# Chapter 12: Manage Your Personal Behavior

*Self-Discipline Is the Best Discipline for a Fire Service Leader*

Organizational discipline is a topic that most folks don't want to deal with as either a supervisor or subordinate. There is, however, a great deal of interest and thirst for information that will help the leaders within an agency to be consistent, fair, transparent and honest when forced to activate the disciplinary process.

Whenever I discuss the privileges and pitfalls of taking on the mantel of leadership, the disciplinary process is always a topic of great interest and discussion. Most folks say they are very uncomfortable "sitting in judgment," as it were, of other members, but understand the organizational need to maintain discipline. The discussions usually go something like this: "Being a company (or battalion or division) commander is the best job I've ever had, except for the fact that I am expected to instill and manage the disciplinary process. I work hard to keep myself out of trouble and my nose clean, but I have to investigate situations and deliver punishment when it is needed. A large part of my working day is spent on discipline issues instead of doing real work. If it weren't for this aspect of my position, I could get at least another meaningful drill in each work week. I dislike that part of my job and wish someone else could handle it for me."

My only response to these brave men and women is "welcome to the club." Some of the work that leadership involves isn't as pleasant as the emergency response part. Let me say loud and clear that the best discipline I know of is self-discipline. Members should have the opportunity to learn the rules and regulations of the department as part of their recruit training and orientation process. In fact, the important rules need to be reviewed on the first day on the job. Many organizations have packaged the dozen or so critical rules into one document. This information helps to get you through your career. Once reviewed, the agency expects its members to follow the rules (this is simple but often overlooked). It seems to me that the best fire-rescue officers and members are the ones that have self control and self discipline, on and off the job.

Fire and EMS agencies must start with the best possible employee/member attainable. If you are in the intolerable position of hiring folks with sordid and questionable backgrounds, your agency will likely spend a disproportionate amount of time and energy delivering discipline and then on to court to defend your actions.

Let me give you the best advice I can: hire the best candidates with known and validated clean backgrounds. We are in a great position of having so many people interested in becoming firefighter/EMTs that you should consider hiring or recruiting only the very best that your community has to offer. Don't short change your selection and qualification process, make it the most robust selection system you can afford! This is the period when you can avoid the headache of letting problem people enter your workforce or membership. If a person was fired from another job or dishonorably discharged (to include less then honorable discharge) from the military, it is likely that person will not work in your outfit. The best quote I ever heard on this topic is from a nationally recognized lecturer, Retired Commander Gordon Graham of the California Highway Patrol: "Past performance will predict future behavior." Pick the best and brightest candidates for public safety positions and never settle for questionable people. Your life will be a lot easier and your department a lot better for the effort.

It can be argued that a firefighter in this country has more authority than a police officer (cops hate hearing me say this). Relating to behavior, understand that we are never off duty. I know it may not seem appropriate, or even fair, that fire departments must have concerns about a member's off-duty behavior. But the truth is, some of our members get into a lot of trouble away from the firehouse.

Let's examine the evidence. When a firefighter responds to a medical emergency that requires injuries to be exposed to determine their extent and to deliver treatment, firefighters are expected to cut clothing away from a person's body. When a person dials 9-1-1 and requests assistance, firefighters can enter the person's home without a search warrant. Many times, sick or injured people are home alone and their possessions are in plain sight. The belief is that the firefighter cutting away the clothing or assisting a person sick at home will not violate the highest level of public trust. All of us, career and volunteer members alike, must have this level of public trust to perform our jobs. If a firefighter robs a bank, beats a spouse, threatens workplace violence or misuses a weapon, it is difficult to get the public to buy into placing all of the necessary trust into the department. Off-duty behavior is just as important as on-duty conduct if we are to maintain our value to those we are sworn to protect.

After a negative event occurs involving our members, the newspaper headline or television news tease starts with the fact that "A firefighter from..." was connected to a crime. It also generally is pointed out if the person was a previous member or a retired member, so pick your staff carefully. It is easy to take exception to the way the media covers stories involving fire and EMS members, but the reality is that a higher standard is expected of public officials who hold positions of trust in our society.

Knowing that the public is demanding a higher level of behavior from us, we must meet that challenge or suffer the consequences of our actions. Most departments have structured discipline processes that outline how and when they are implemented. Once negative behavior is observed that must be corrected, a formal process must start and be carried out fairly and honestly every time for everybody in the system, no exceptions. The expressed goal should be for the system to correct behavior and to do the least amount of damage to the member and the department. This is always a balancing act and adds a significant measure of stress to the folks who must implement the system.

Let me remind you to do your department and yourself a favor and select the best folks to become members (never just settle). Next, try to instill self-discipline at all levels of your department. Finally, have a solid discipline system that is fair, open, transparent, consistent, and honest.

# Chapter 13:
# Be Nice

*Exploring a Pillar of Great Fire Department Customer Service*

It is interesting to reflect on the fact that some aspects of the fire and EMS world are constantly becoming more complicated. When I think back to 1971, when I started in our business as a recruit firefighter/EMT, fire station life was fairly simple. Much of the life-saving technology we take for granted today did not exist. But some things have not changed, and this section will explore one of the pillars of great customer service: simply to "Be Nice."

The history of "being nice" leads back to the writings and teachings of Chief Brunacini. Chief "Bruno" can go on for hours discussing the impacts and effects that simply being "nice" to our members and our customers can have on our departments and ourselves. No leadership book on personal rules of behavior and conduct would be complete without making mention of this golden rule – "be nice."

The goal of every fire-rescue department should be to be a high performance, high trust agency known for its fairness, openness and transparency, and where good personnel morale is important to all. "Being nice" takes on a very significant role when it comes to reaching these benchmarks. The core value of "being nice" becomes the basis or foundation of reaching the lofty goal described above.

To put this concept into practice, think of the meanest kid in your neighborhood. Now, go on a virtual trip with me to the mean kid's house and knock on his or her door. Who is most likely to open the door? My sense is that it will be a mean mom or dad or perhaps a mean older sibling. By now, you have caught onto the idea that mean people are living in that imaginary home. The point that I want to make is that the mean kid has to learn how to be mean from someone and that it is typically mom, dad, or older brothers and sisters.

The fire chief expects high quality and trustworthy performance from all department members, all of the time, and under all conditions. Although a call may be the 10th or 15th response of the shift, it is the first one for the affected individual. In most cases, it is the first and only time they have dialed 9-1-1 for our help. The chief needs (and perhaps should demand) the members to "be nice" to all of the customers all of the time. Therefore, the chief must be supportive of the members who answer the calls all hours of the day and night and under all conditions. Using the mean-kid theory, if the chief treats people in a mean way or if the organization is not supportive of the troops, it is a real stretch of the imagination to think that the firefighters will go out and "be nice" under those circumstances. Actually, the outfit is most likely to receive citizens' complaints about poor performance and the negative attitude displayed by the workforce. Conversely, if the department supports and treats the workforce nicely, it's more likely that the firefighters will meet or exceed the challenges that you put before them in the most professional way.

The next part of "being nice" is to remind your troops that they must "be nice" first. The organizational expectation is that our folks should "be nice" to other members and customers as the interactions are initiated, not waiting for the other party to "be nice" first. It is amazing how many negative issues can be avoided if the interaction starts off on a positive footing. We must remember that our customers are generally having a really bad day before dialing 9-1-1 and they typically have very little experience with emergency events. On the other hand, resolving emergencies and not adding stress to the customer's day is our vocation or avocation when we pin on the badge.

The department should have a set of empowering rules (Image 1 and 2). Members should feel empowered and supported to "be nice" to one another and to our customers. In organizations that are well supported, the list of "success stories" about conveying acts of kindness is just about endless with tales of matching departmental support from budget dollars to private donations to the old standby, a simple "Thank You!"

Several fire departments produce a quarterly "Great News" book that is a collection of dozens of thank-you notes and cards received during the previous 90 days. This publication is shipped to the mayor, city council and local media, giving these external stakeholders some idea of what is happening inside their organization. The "Great News" book is added to the department's website so that their membership and others can quickly access the information.

Some departments have a customer service award process that recognizes members for going above and beyond to "be nice." These types of programs should never interfere with the various types of recognition programs that are in place for fire, medical and rescue personnel; rather, "being nice" should be an embellishment of a departmental awards program.

The first part of "being nice" and high-quality customer service is being able to perform your job flawlessly. Nothing can replace being a high performance emergency medical technician, paramedic and/or firefighter. Know your job inside and out and do it well, every time. "Being nice" will be a major added bonus for you, your department, and the citizens and visitors who call on you.

"Be Nice"

Thanks for taking the time to read this book. If you are interested, please be sure to check out my site at ChiefRubin.com and follow me on Twitter @ChiefRubin

Remember to be careful out there.

Copyright © 2013
Dennis L. Rubin All rights reserved.
ISBN: 098545203X
ISBN-13: 978-0985452032

V 2.1

19557421R00036

Made in the USA
Charleston, SC
31 May 2013